A Simple Guide
of
Catholic Terms

All booklets are published thanks to the generous support of the members of the Catholic Truth Society

CATHOLIC TRUTH SOCIETY
PUBLISHERS TO THE HOLY SEE

A Simple Glossary of Catholic Terms

Like every family, the Catholic Church has a lot of special words and phrases which have a clear and concise meaning to Catholics, but can be very puzzling to others. This word-list is intended to explain some of our curious family words and usages. It is no substitute for the *Catholic Encyclopaedia*, or for theological and Scriptural dictionaries – indeed the terms of theology have not been included here – but it might help clear up confusion. Words relating to the Church of the past have also been included, because even if the things they describe (like "Prime" or "maniples") are at present not in use, readers will benefit from completeness. Surely, there will be words we have forgotten to include, but we have tried to think of all the important ones, and quite a lot of unimportant but amusing ones as well.

A

Abba (Aramaic, "father"), familiar name used by Jesus for his Father; later the affectionate title given to senior *monks* in Egypt; from this derives **Abbot**, the superior of a *Monastery* of men, and Abbess, the equivalent for women. In either case the *monastery* can be called an Abbey. The French title abbé is used out of courtesy for junior *clergy*, because before the Revolution the position and income of an abbot was often given to young men to finance their studies.

Absolution (Latin *ABSOLVO*, "set free"), the solemn pronouncement by a *Priest* that someone's sins are forgiven, in the *Sacrament* of *Penance*.

Abstinence (Latin *ABSTINENTIA*, from *ABSTINEO*, "hold back, refrain"), not eating meat; a form of penance now obligatory in England and Wales only on *Ash Wednesday* and *Good Friday*, and binding only on those between the ages of 14 and 65. In the past, Catholics were bound to abstain from meat on every Friday throughout the year. In some other countries this is still the custom. Eating fish instead of meat on days of abstinence is a traditional, not obligatory, practice, one which finds Scriptural support in John 21:9-14.

Acolyte (Greek AKOLYTES, "follower"), originally the fourth grade of *Holy Orders*, now suspended in the Latin Church. Now used for a lay ministry, assistant to the *priest*, hardly ever conferred except for those on the way to *ordination* as *Deacon* or *Priest*. Used also to refer to boys who serve at *Mass*.

Act, a movement of the will and heart towards God, hence an impulse in *prayer*. Specifically *Acts* can mean short prayers designed to express the will to some virtue, most commonly an *Act of Contrition*, the *prayer* used during *Confession* to express sorrow for sin, but also *Acts of Faith, Hope and Charity* are found in *prayer*-books.

Advent (Latin ADVENTUS, "arrival"), the *season* before *Christmas*, celebrating the coming of Christ to earth at Bethlehem, and in the *Church*, and at the Day of Judgement; traditionally a time of *penance*.

Agnus Dei (Latin, "lamb of God"), a text used just before *Communion* at *Mass*, often set to music.

Alb (Latin TUNICA ALBA, "white garment"), the second of the *Vestments* for *Mass*, a full-length white sleeved gown. Sometimes also used for servers at *Mass*.

Alleluia verse, a joyous chant sung just before the *Gospel* at *Mass*, except during *Lent*.

All Saints, a *Solemnity* on 1st November each year to commemorate the countless saints who have no particular day. Formerly "All Hallows". The vigil of the feast, beginning on the evening before, October 31st, was known as Halloween (All Hallows' Eve). Once a pre-Christian pagan festival, it has since become a secular event featuring ghosts, witches and spirits.

All Souls, a commemoration on 2nd November for all those who have died, to pray for their souls.

Almsgiving, practical charitable donations to those in need, either in money or goods.

Almuce, middle-English variant of the word Amice and the term used for *mozetta*, a fur-lined shoulder cape worn by *canons*.

Altar (Latin *ALTARE* from *ALTUS* "high"), a strong oblong flat raised surface, ideally of stone on a stone base, used for the Sacrifice of the *Mass*. It is "dressed" with three white altar-cloths, running its full length and hanging down at the ends, and an altar-frontal, covering the side facing the people, properly of the colour of the *season*.

Altar-bread, the wafers of unleavened bread used for the *Eucharist*.

Altar Missal, see *Missal*, *Sacramentary*.

Altar-rails, low railings of metal, stone or wood, found in some churches, serving to demarcate the *sanctuary*, and to provide support for those kneeling to receive *Communion*.

Altar of Repose, a side altar, or a specially constructed occasional altar, decorated to serve as a place of *reservation* of the *Blessed Sacrament* for the evening of *Maundy Thursday*.

Ambo (Greek AMBON, "pulpit" from ANABAINO, "go up steps"), a raised platform in the *Sanctuary* where the Gospel is proclaimed; also sometimes used for preaching from. Originally a term from the Greek-speaking Church of the East. See also *Lectern*.

Amice, the first of the *Vestments* for *Mass*, a neck-cloth to keep the *alb* clean and cover the *priest*'s collar.

Anchorites (Greek ANA CHORITES, "not joining in the singing"), those who live lives of complete solitude devoted to *prayer*, remaining in a single place for life. (Now rare.)

Angelus (Latin "angel"), a *prayer* commemorating the *annunciation* by the Angel to Mary, traditionally said at six in the morning, midday and six in the evening, hence the Angelus Bell which is rung at those times.

Annunciation (Latin *ANNUNTIO*, "announce"), a *Solemnity* on 25th March to commemorate the announcement of the Angel to Mary that she would give birth to Jesus (Lk 1:26-38); during Christian times was kept as the first day of the year; known in England as *Lady Day*.

Anointing, smearing blessed oil on the skin, usually on the forehead, as a sign of healing and strengthening. Used in *Baptism* and *Confirmation*, in the *Ordination* of *priests* and *bishops*, and *Anointing of the sick*, all of which are *Sacraments*.

Anointing of the Sick, a *Sacrament* for healing, which should be given at the onset of any serious illness, and may be repeated.

Antiphon (Greek *ANTI* "opposite", *PHONÉ* "voice"), a verse usually derived from Scripture, sung before and after every Psalm in the *Divine Office*, varying according to the day and *season*. Hence **Antiphonale**, a book containing the chants for the *Antiphons* and the rest of the *Office*.

Apostolic Tradition, the Church's belief that the faith she passes on comes down from the Apostles in an unbroken succession guaranteed by the Holy Spirit; and that the Scriptures can only properly be proclaimed and interpreted within the Church. Even where the words and formulae used to express the Church's faith have been refined and developed throughout her history, *Apostolic Tradition* means that this fullness of belief is already latent from the very earliest Christian times, being entrusted to the Apostles and their successors by Jesus Christ himself.

Archbishop, the *bishop* of an important *diocese*, acting as the leader of a group of *Dioceses* or a *Province*. Also known as a *Metropolitan*.

Ascension, commemoration of when Jesus "withdrew from them (his apostles) and was carried up to heaven" some time after his resurrection. **Ascension Thursday**, forty days after Easter, the *solemnity* commemorating the ascension of Jesus (Ac 1:6-11).

Ashes, the dust of burnt *Palms* often mixed with water and smeared on the foreheads of the faithful as a sign of accepting *Penance* at the beginning of *Lent*. Hence **Ash Wednesday**, six and a half weeks before *Easter*, the first day of *Lent*.

Assumption, a *Solemnity* on 15th August to commemorate the triumph of Mary entering heaven as a sign of hope for us (Rv 12:1-6).

Augustinians, members of a family of *friars* or *nuns* inspired by the example of St Augustine, also most communities of *Canons Regular*.

Ave Maria (Latin, "Hail, Mary"), the most popular *prayer* to the Virgin Mary, composed of words from Scripture.

B

Baldacchino, architectural term for a stone-built canopy over an *altar*, often curtained around. Also called a *Ciborium*.

Baptism (Greek BAPTIZO, "dip"), dipping water and pouring it over the head, or immersing the person in water, the *sacrament* by which new Christians are made members of the *Church*; preceded by one *anointing* as a sign of healing, and followed by another as a sign of strength.

Baptism of the Lord, a *Solemnity* kept on the Sunday after *Epiphany* to commemorate the baptism of Jesus in the Jordan.

Baptistery, the area of the *church* used for *Baptism*, containing the *Font*, ideally a demarcated space near the main door from which the *procession* can move to the *Sanctuary* after *Baptism*.

Benedicite (Latin, "bless ye"), the canticle of the Three Young Men (Dn 3:29-68), used at *Lauds* on Sundays and feast-days.

Benedictines, *monks* or *nuns* following the Rule of St Benedict, usually wearing black.

Benediction, a service of worship centered around the *Blessed Sacrament*, exposed on the *altar* in a *monstrance*; may be accompanied by hymns, silent *prayer*, readings or the *Divine Office*.

Benedictus (Latin "blessed"), the canticle of Zechariah (Lk 1:68-79), used at *Lauds*.

Benedictus (ii), the second half of the *Sanctus*, sometimes detached and set to music separately.

Bidding Prayers, term used in England for the *Prayer of the Faithful*, intercessions made after the *sermon* at *Mass*.

Biretta (Italian), a square stiff cap with three wings on top, formerly worn by *clergy* in the *Sanctuary* (it is not street dress); red for *cardinals*, purple for *prelates*, black for others; now rare. *Secular clergy* have a pom-pom on top of it.

Bishop (Greek *EPISKOPOS*, "overseer"), a *priest* chosen and *consecrated* or *ordained* to administer a *diocese*, and to confer *confirmation* and *ordinations*.

Blackfriars, traditional English name for *Dominicans*.

Blessed Sacrament, generally, the *Eucharist*; particularly used to refer to the consecrated *Host* reserved as a focus for devotion - such as contemplative prayer before the *Tabernacle*, in *processions*, *Benediction* and so on.

Breviary, a book containing all the texts for the *Divine Office*.

Bull (Latin *BULLA*, "seal"), a formal document from the *Pope* making a declaration of some importance, sealed with a leaden seal.

Burse (French *BOURSE*, Latin *BURSA*, "purse"), a square fabric-covered container for the *corporal*, not now always used, but if it is, it should match the *chalice*-veil and *chasuble*.

C

Camaldolese, an *order* of *monks* living strictly as *hermits* within a community.

Candlemas, traditional English name for the feast of the *Purification* of Mary, or the *Presentation of Jesus*, on 2nd February.

Canon (Greek *KANON*, "rule"), a decree on some matter of *Church* order or discipline passed by the *Pope* or a General Council which is binding on the *Church* unless revoked by the same authority, collected into the **Code of Canon Law**, and interpreted by **Canon Lawyers**.

Canon (ii), derived from the above, originally a man whose way of life is regulated by the *canons*, hence one of a community of *priests*; later divided into **Canons Regular** who take *vows* and live almost like *monks*, and **Canons Secular** who can own their own property. These formed communities at *Cathedrals*, so that the title *Canon* came to mean one of the senior *Cathedral clergy*, now often given as an honorary title.

Canon (iii), the central *prayer* of the *Mass*, or *Eucharistic Prayer*.

Canon of Scripture, the complete list of 72 (or 73 if Jeremiah and Lementations are counted as two) books included in sacred scriptures by the *Apostolic Tradition*.

Canopy (Greek *KONOPEION*, "mosquito net"), a fabric shade carried on four poles over the *Blessed Sacrament* during outdoor *processions*, e.g. on *Corpus Christi*.

Cardinal, a senior dignitary of the Church, one of the College who elect a new *Pope* after the death of his predecessor. Technically they do this as senior clergy of the *Diocese* of Rome electing their *Bishop*; for this reason each Cardinal is assigned a titular Church within the Diocese of Rome. Cardinals are now usually *Archbishops*, either resident in Rome and working within the Curia (the administrative offices of the *Holy See*), or governing their Dioceses throughout the world.

Carmelites, members of a large family of *friars* or *nuns* inspired by the example of the early *hermits* on Mount Carmel in Palestine, with a strong tradition of *prayer*. Known in England as *Whitefriars* because of the white outer cloaks they wear in public.

Carthusians, an *order* of *monks* or *nuns* founded by St Bruno, living strictly as *hermits* but within a community.

Cassock (Persian *kazagand*, "long coat"), a full-length sleeved garment, buttoned down the front, worn as the basic foundation garment for all *vestments*, and in many *religious* communities as the ordinary house dress. May be girded with a *fascia*. Colours of fabric, buttons and *fascia* vary according to rank; white for the *Pope*, red for *Cardinals*, purple for *bishops* and *monsignors*; otherwise black.

Catechumen, a new convert to Christianity who is under instruction but has not yet been *baptized*. Hence **Catechumenate**, the period of instruction for new Christians, not to be confused with receiving existing Christians into full *Communion* with the *Church*.

Catenians, (Latin CATENA, "chain") an association of Catholic men (often working in the professions or in business) and their wives, who meet for mutual support, prayer, and charitable purposes. It was founded in Manchester in 1908, and counts 11,000 members worldwide.

Cathedral (Greek KATHEDRA, "seat"), the mother *Church* of a *diocese* where the *Bishop* takes his seat; usually but not necessarily a large *church*.

Catholic Womens' League, a charitable association of women devoted to *evangelization* and practical works of charity.

Celibacy (Latin COELEBS, "bachelor"), technically the state of not yet being married, but by extension the condition of *priests*, *monks*, *friars* and *nuns* and all who are committed to remaining unmarried and consequently continent and chaste.

Censer, or *thurible*, a metal container suspended from chains, used for burning *incense*.

Chalice (Latin CALIX, "cup"), a cup of gold or gilt silver, used for the wine which is to be *consecrated* at *Mass*.

Chapel, either a partially separated section of a *church* with an *altar* in it (side-altar in side-chapel), or a free-standing building which does not serve a *parish* but only a small community.

Chaplet, a loop of beads, on which various forms of *prayer* can be recited, the best-known being the *Rosary*.

Chapter, originally the daily meeting of *monks* at which one *chapter* of the Rule was read before business; later similar meetings of *canons*; hence the business of the meeting itself, and the *canons* seen as a legislative body.

Charism (Greek CHARISMA, "gift of grace"), a gift of the Holy Spirit given to a specific person for a specific purpose, hence the sense of purpose and spiritual identity of that person, or of a group of persons, e.g. a *Religious Order*.

Charterhouse (French place name, *CHARTREUSE*), a *monastery* of *Carthusians*.

Chastity, the virtue of sexual self-restraint. For the married this means fidelity to their spouse, with due respect for each other and the law of God. For the unmarried this means *continence*: abstaining from deliberate sexual activity.

Chasuble, the sixth of the *Vestments* for *Mass*, an all-enveloping sleeveless garment which covers the others as a symbol of charity. It forms a set with the *stole* etc, and is of different colours for different *seasons*.

Christ the King, the last Sunday before *Advent*, a *Solemnity* to remind us that no earthly king or government can claim our loyalty, above that of Christ alone our true King.

Christening, old English term for *Baptism*, stressing that the person being baptized is now a Christian.

Christmas, the *Solemnity* commemorating the birth of Jesus at Bethlehem, extending to the Christmas *Octave*, the eight days until 1st January, and the Christmas Season until the Sunday after *Epiphany*, although it traditionally extended for 40 days until *Candlemas* (2 February).

Church (Greek *KYRIAKON*, "the Lord's place"), the entire community of all faithful Christians, united through space and time, with the *Pope* as the earthly focus of unity, and Christ alone as head. Formed by the *Eucharist*, and thus known as the *Mystical Body of Christ*. There can only be one *Church* in this sense of the word.

Church (ii), a "local" *church* as expression of the universal *Church*, with the *bishop* as focus of unity; effectively the same as a *diocese*.

Church (iii), a building set aside and consecrated to be used for worship alone.

Ciborium (i) (Latin *CIBUM*, "food"), an airtight container, usually shaped like a covered cup, for the *Blessed Sacrament*; used to contain hosts during Mass, before and after their consecration, and *reserved* in the *Tabernacle*.

Ciborium (ii), architectural term for a stone-built canopy over an altar, often curtained around. Also known as a *Baldacchino*.

Cincture (Latin *CINCTURA*, "girding"), the third of the *Vestments* for *Mass*, a doubled cord to gird up the *alb* and hold the *stole* in place.

Circumcision, traditional name for the *Solemnity* on 1st January, reminding us that Jesus was a Jew in obedience to the Old Law. Also known as "*Octave* of *Christmas*", now as the *Solemnity of Mary, Mother of God*.

Cistercians (French place name, *CÎTEAUX*), *monks* or *nuns* following the Rule of St Benedict in a strict manner, centrally organised; wearing white.

Clergy (Greek *KLÉROS*, "lot"), those men chosen by God to serve Him and His people, set aside by *ordination*, and with various duties and responsibilities.

Clerk (Latin *CLERICUS*, "*clergyman*"), a man in *Holy Orders*; Clerks Regular are members of a *religious order* which has *vows*, but also a *mission* to the world, the *Jesuits* being the best-known.

Collect, a *prayer* led by the *priest* to collect, gather together the intentions of the people, in the *Mass* it comes after the *Kyrie* and *Gloria*.

Communion, Holy, the act of receiving and consuming the Body and Blood of Christ under the form of the consecrated *host* and the consecrated wine, usually at Mass. See *Eucharist*.

Communion verse, a chant sung while *Communion* is being distributed at *Mass*.

Compline, or Night Prayer, the last hour of the *Divine Office* at the end of the day.

Conclave (Latin CUM CLAVE, "with a key"), the "locked-up" assembly of *Cardinals* charged with electing a new *Pope*.

Confession, the admission of guilt and asking forgiveness for sins, the necessary precondition for receiving *Absolution* in the *Sacrament* of *Penance*.

Confessor, a *priest* who hears *Confession* in the *Sacrament* of *Penance*.

Confessor (ii), a saint who is not a *martyr* but "confesses" his or her faith by the example of life; e.g. St Edward, King and Confessor, so-called to distinguish him from his great uncle St Edward, King and Martyr.

Confirmation, the *anointing* on the forehead of young Christians to ratify their *Baptism* and strengthen them for their work as Christians, properly conferred by a *Bishop*.

Congregation (Latin CONGREGATIO, "flocking together"), a gathering of people in a *church*.

Congregation (ii), a community e.g. of *priests* living together.

Congregation (iii), a major department or *dicastery* of the *Holy See*, usually based in the *Vatican* City.

Consecrate (Latin CON SACRARE, "make holy together"), the act of handing over some person or thing over to God for His exclusive use. Hence **Consecration**, the central part of the *Mass*, when the bread and wine are consecrated to form the *Eucharist*.

Consistory (Latin CUM SISTO, "stand together"), a meeting of *Cardinals* with the *Pope*, particularly when new *Cardinals* are created.

Contemplation, a form of mental *prayer* without words and without thought, being still in the presence of God. "He looks at me and I look at Him." Hence **Contemplative**, particularly applied to members of *religious orders* devoted to *prayer*.

Continence, abstaining from deliberate sexual activity, naturally expected of the unmarried.

Convent (Latin CONVENTUS, "community"), a *religious* community house; in England mainly used for houses of female *religious* or *nuns*.

Cope (Latin *CAPA* "cloak with hood"), a full-length open cloak, with a rudimentary hood, usually worn over a *cassock* and *surplice* for ceremonies other than *Mass*, such as weddings, *processions* and *Benediction*.

Corporal (Latin *CORPUS*, "body"), a square white cloth unfolded on the *altar* to hold the *chalice* and *paten* during *Mass*. It may be stored in a *burse* until it is needed.

Corpus Christi (Latin, "Body of Christ"), the Thursday after *Trinity Sunday*, a *Solemnity* to celebrate the gift of the *Eucharist*, marked with *processions* and solemn *Benediction*, now moved to be celebrated on the nearest Sunday.

Cotta (Italian, "cut short"), a shortened form of the *surplice*, used by boys over a *cassock* to serve *Mass*.

Council, a meeting of *bishops* to discuss matters of Christian doctrine, morals and discipline. *Councils* may be local, consisting of *bishops* from a particular nation or region, sometimes known as a *Synod*, or they may involve all the *bishops* of the world in a General Council, also called an *Ecumenical Council* (Greek *OIKOUMENÉ*, "inhabited world"). The doctrinal decisions of a General Council may be formally defined and thus become part of the *Deposit of Faith*; pastoral and disciplinary decisions are for their own time only and can be changed later.

Creed (Latin CREDO, "I believe"), a text setting out the articles of Catholic faith; the best-known are the Apostles' Creed, used at *Baptism*, and the Nicene Creed, used at *Mass*.

Crosier, or *pastoral staff*, a long staff of metal or wood, topped with a curled head like a shepherd's crook, carried by *bishops* and *abbots* as a symbol of their pastoral care.

Cruets, small glass or metal jugs to contain wine and water for use at *Mass*.

Curate (French CURÉ, Latin CURATUS, one with responsibility for the care of souls), used in English to mean a junior or assistant *priest*.

CWL, the *Catholic Womens' League*.

D

Dalmatic (Latin TUNICA DALMATICA, "Balkan-style garment"), a three-quarter length closed garment with short wide sleeves, matching the *chasuble*, worn by the *Deacon* at *Mass*. Also worn by the *bishop* under his *chasuble* on solemn occasions.

Deacon (Greek *DIAKONOS*, "servant"), a man *ordained* to serve and assist the *Church*.

Dean (Latin *DECANUS*, "controller of ten"), a *priest* chosen to serve a collection of *priests*, either living in community or at least nominally so, as the *Dean* of a *Cathedral* or of a *Chapter* is responsible for the *canons*; and the *Dean* of a Deanery (in America a Vicar Forane) cares for about ten parishes as a subdivision of a *Diocese*.

Deposit of Faith, the body of teaching entrusted to us through the *Church* of past ages, and which we must guard (1 Tm 6:20), although it develops and grows as the *Church* grows. See also *Tradition*.

Dicastery (Greek *DIKASTERION*, "place where justice is done"), general term for any department of the administration of the *Holy See*.

Diocese (Greek *DI'OIKEIA*, "around the house"), an area of territory administered for *Church* purposes by a *Bishop*, possessing a *Cathedral*; also known as a Local Church. The *diocese* was an administrative region of the late Roman Empire which survived in the *Church* long after the Empire had fallen.

Discipline, small whip of cord, once used as means of voluntary *penance*.

Divine Mercy, a devotion celebrating the love of God, often made on the Sunday after *Easter*; originating in Poland.

Divine Office, the round of prayers for different times of the day used by *monks*, *nuns*, and *priests*, and now often by *lay people* as well; well known elements being *Matins, Lauds, Vespers* and *Compline*. The full Office also used to include the *Little Hours*, (*Prime*, *Terce*, *Sext*, *None*) now *Prayer during the Day*. See *Midday prayer*.

Divine Praises, a series of short invocations of God and the Saints, commonly repeated after *Benediction*.

Doctor of the Church, a saint whose learning and writings have made a significant contribution to the development of Christian doctrine.

Dominicans, members of a large family of *friars* or *nuns* inspired by the example of St Dominic, in particular with a *mission* to *preach* and write. In England known as *Blackfriars* because they wear black outer cloaks.

E

Easter, greatest feast in the Christian calendar, marking the death and resurrection of Jesus and the promise of new life. Celebrations begin with the *Triduum* at the end of *Holy Week*, marking the end of the 40 days of *Lent* and the beginning of the 50 days of Eastertide until *Pentecost*. In the northern hemisphere, celebrated on the first Sunday after the first full moon of spring.

Easter Vigil, a *Liturgy* of *prayer*, scripture and singing during the night before *Easter* Sunday, including the blessing of the Paschal Candle, celebration of *Baptism*, and ending with *Mass*.

Easter Week, from *Easter* Sunday to *Low Sunday*.

Election, Rite of, a ceremony to welcome *Catechumens* who are in the last stages of preparation for *Baptism*, sometimes celebrated publicly before the *bishop* in *Lent*.

Embolism (Greek EMBOLOS "stopper"), curious name for the *prayer* at *Mass* after the Our Father, so called because the prayer had been inserted into the *canon* of the *mass*.

Encyclical (Greek *ENKYKLO* "in a circle"), a circular letter from the *Pope* addressed to the whole world, setting out some important teaching at some length. Usually known by the first two words of its text in Latin.

Epiclesis (Greek, "calling down"), that part of a *Eucharistic Prayer* in which the Holy Spirit is invoked to come down on the offerings of bread and wine to transform them.

Epiphany (Greek *EPI-PHANEIA*, "make manifest"), the *Solemnity* on 6th January commemorating the manifestation of Jesus to the world, at the visit of the Magi, his *Baptism* in the Jordan, and the Marriage at Cana. Traditionally followed by the *Season* of *Epiphany*, meditating on these themes until just before *Lent*.

Epistle (Latin *EPISTOLA* "letter"), traditional name for the first reading at *Mass*, which usually came from an *Epistle*, (letter) of St Paul; traditionally read from the right hand side of the altar, as the people see it.

Eucharist, the Mass, (Greek, *EUKHARISTIA*, "giving thanks"), the sacrament of the Body and Blood of Jesus Christ under the form of bread and wine, consecrated at *Mass* by the priest who represents Christ to his *Church*. Receiving *Holy Communion* at Mass allows the Christian faithful truly to become the Body of Christ, the *Church*.

Eucharistic Prayer, the central *prayer* of the *Mass*, incorporating an *Epiclesis* and the *Consecration*.

Ecumenism (Greek *OIKOUMENÉ*, "inhabited world"), the movement which began in earnest after the Second Vatican Council attempting to bring all Christians into closer unity.

Evangelization (Greek *EUANGELIZO*, "bring good news"), the process of introducing people to the truths of the *Gospel*, an essential part of *Mission*.

Evening Prayer, alternative name for *Vespers*.

Exorcist (Greek *EX ORKIZO*, "adjure"), originally the third grade of *Holy Orders*, now suspended in the Latin Church. The ministry of Exorcism, delivering people or places from malign or demonic influences, is now entrusted only to a senior *priest* of notable common sense and stability.

Exposition of the Blessed Sacrament, placing the consecrated *Eucharist* in a *monstrance* and displaying it for adoration.

F

Fascia, part of vestments for Mass; a wide cloth band used to gird the *cassock*, hanging down on the left, often with tassels.

Fast, Eucharistic, total abstention from food and drink for one hour before receiving *Holy Communion*; traditionally practised from the previous midnight.

Fasting, self-discipline in matters of food. Traditionally, on a fast-day only one meal was permitted, with two light snacks. Although fast days were once very numerous, including much of *Lent* and *Advent*, Catholics in England and Wales are now obliged to fast only on *Ash Wednesday* and *Good Friday*, which are also days of *abstinence*. Fasting is binding on those in good health over 18 and under 60. Many people fast on other days (such as Fridays during *Lent*) as a voluntary *penance*.

Fathers of the Church, the great writers and preachers who helped form the *Church* particularly during the fourth and fifth centuries.

Fátima, village, now a major Marian shrine, in Portugal associated with the apparition of the Virgin Mary to three youngsters in 1917. Commemorated on 13th May.

Feast-days, the middle rank of special days, for major saints and some aspects of the life of Jesus.

Feria, (Latin *FERIA* "holiday") curiously in the Church an ordinary weekday that is not a holiday, where there is no saint's day or other commemoration.

Ferraiuola (Italian), a cloak of light fabric, worn on ceremonial occasions over the *cassock* and *fascia*, usually black, but purple for *prelates* and red for the *Pope*.

Font (Latin *FONS*, "fountain'), a large basin, usually of stone, containing the water used for *Baptism*, and sited in the *Baptistery* of a church.

Footpace, the platform in front of an *altar* where the *priest* stands during *Mass*.

Forty Hours, the ceremony of *Exposition* of the *Blessed Sacrament* for two and a half day's adoration, ending with *Benediction*, usually accompanied by other devotions.

Fraction (Latin *FRACTIO*, "breaking"), the breaking of the consecrated *Host* before *Communion* at *Mass*.

Franciscans, members of many families of *friars* or *nuns* inspired by the example of St Francis of Assisi, in particular his dedication to "Lady *Poverty*". *Franciscans* are easily distinguished by wearing a knotted rope around their waists. In England known as *Greyfriars* because they wear brown *habits*.

Friar (old French FRÈRE, "brother"), a man vowed to *religious* life as a travelling preacher, under *vows* of *poverty*, *chastity* and *obedience*, organized in an international *order*; living in a **Friary** but often moving from one to another.

G

Galera, or "soup-plate hat", a round hat with a broad brim, now rarely seen; *Cardinals* had red *galere* with fifteen tassels on each side, other ranks varying colours and varying numbers of tassels. Properly worn as street dress.

Gaudete Sunday, the third Sunday of *Advent*, when the *Introit* begins Gaudete, "rejoice", and the sombre colour of the *vestments* is lightened to a delicate rose.

Genuflect (Latin "knee" and "bend"), gesture of respect when passing in front of the *Blessed Sacrament*, kneeling briefly on the right knee. Traditionally if the *Blessed Sacrament* is exposed, one kneels on both knees.

Gloria (Latin "glory"), a hymn of praise used at *Mass* on feasts and solemnities after the *Kyrie*, often set to music.

Good Friday, the Friday before *Easter* Sunday, commemorating the triumph of Jesus on the Cross. Marked by singing the *Passion* and honouring the Cross. See *Triduum*.

Gospel (Old English GOD SPEL, "good news"), at *Mass* the reading from one of the four Gospels which concludes the *Liturgy* of the Word. Also preaching the content of Christ's life and teaching as recorded in the four Gospels and commented on in the New Testament letters.

Gradine (Latin GRADUS, "step"), a step or shelf running along the back of traditional altar, which may serve to hold candles, flowers or reliquaries. Not available when altars are free-standing.

Gradual, a slow chant traditionally sung in preparation for the *Gospel* at *Mass*. Hence **Graduale**, a book containing that and other chants for the *Mass*.

Great O Antiphons, for the last week before *Christmas* the *Magnificat* at *Vespers* is introduced with a particularly elaborate antiphon, each one beginning with O; the last is "O Emmanuel". The hymn "O come, O come, Emmanuel" translates them.

Greyfriars, traditional English name for *Franciscans*.

Guadalupe, village in Mexico and now a Marian shrine, associated with the apparition of the Virgin Mary to Juan Diego in 1531. Commemorated on 13th December.

H

Habit (Latin *HABITUS*, "costume"), the distinctive garb of a member of a *religious order*.

Hermits (Greek *ERÉMIA* OR *EREMOS*, "deserted or solitary"), those who live a life dedicated to *prayer* on their own. May be grouped into communities with some degree of common life, like *Carthusians* and *Camaldolese*.

Holy Days of Obligation, solemn feasts of the Church falling on weekdays when all Catholics are obliged to attend Mass just as they do on a Sunday (and, in theory at least, to abstain from work). A number of these are celebrated by all Catholics everywhere; others apply only in particular countries. The full list of universal Holy Days contains four feasts of *Our Lord*: *Christmas* (25th December), *Epiphany* (6th January), *Ascension* (forty days after Easter), *Corpus Christi* (the Thursday after Trinity Sunday); three of *Our Lady*: the *Mother of God* (1st January), the *Assumption* (15th August), and the *Immaculate Conception* (8th December); and three celebrating the saints: *St Joseph* (19th March), *SS Peter and Paul* (29th June), and *All Saints* (1st November). In England and Wales a number of these solemnities are not observed, or have been transferred to the nearest Sunday; those that are still observed on weekdays are *Christmas*, the *Assumption*, *SS Peter and Paul*, and *All Saints*.

Holy Family, the earthly family of Jesus, usually Jesus, Mary and Joseph, but can be extended to all the cousins mentioned in Scripture. The Feast of the Holy Family is the Sunday after *Christmas*.

Holy Hour, the ceremony of *Exposition* of the *Blessed Sacrament* for one hour's adoration, ending with *Benediction*.

Holy Name, the name of Jesus, celebrated as the name through which we are saved; Feast of the Holy Name now 3rd January.

Holy Office, old name for the Congregation of the Doctrine of the Faith, the *dicastery* of the *Holy See* responsible for accurate teaching. See *Inquisition*.

Holy Saturday, the day before *Easter Sunday*, within the *Triduum*, marked by quiet expectation and austerity, when no *Mass* or *sacraments* are celebrated, in anticipation of the Easter Celebrations, which begin with the *Easter Vigil*. See *Triduum*, and *Easter*.

Holy See, the Papacy. A Bishop's see (from the Latin *SEDES*, "seat") refers both to the diocese he governs and to his authority over it. The Pope, as Bishop of Rome, occupies the See of Rome, which has primacy over all other Christian Churches; it is traditionally called the *Holy See* to mark this. This term can also refer to the various administrative offices (or *dicasteries*) which assist the Pope in different ways. See also *Vatican*.

Holy Week, the last week of *Lent*, beginning with *Palm* (or *Passion*) *Sunday*, a week before *Easter* Sunday; preparation to contemplate and to celebrate the *Easter* mysteries: the passion, death, and resurrection of Jesus, leading to the *Triduum*.

Homily (Greek *HOMILO*, "speak"), a discourse in which the *priest* explains the readings at *Mass*.

Host (Latin *HOSTIA* "sacrificial victim"), the consecrated *Eucharist* in the form of bread; the large *Host* is broken by the *priest* at *Mass*, and small *Hosts* are used to distribute to the people, and to reserve in the *Tabernacle*. Also used casually to mean unconsecrated *altar-breads*.

Humeral veil (Latin *HUMERUS*, "shoulder"), broad band of fabric placed around the shoulders of a *priest* or *deacon* who is carrying the *Blessed Sacrament*, or when giving the blessing at *Benediction*.

I

Immaculate Conception, the understanding that Mary was "chosen before creation began", and prepared by God to be the Mother of Christ, preserved free from Original Sin, and thus able to make a free choice to co-operate with God. Celebrated on 8th December with a *Solemnity*.

Immaculate Heart, the heart of Mary which was totally dedicated to the will of God, as a model for us. Feast of the *Immaculate Heart of Mary*, the day after the *Sacred Heart* of Jesus, 27 June.

Incense, grains of consolidated gum which give off scented smoke when burnt. Used at *Mass* and other ceremonies, to represent the prayers of the saints rising up to heaven. Kept in an incense-boat, and ladled out with an incense-spoon onto glowing charcoal in a *thurible* or *censer*.

Indulgence, either partial or plenary, a papal grant and gift of grace remitting part or all of the temporal punishment due to one's sins; attached conditions will include the sacraments and prayer, and a firm purpose to amend one's life.

Indult, a letter from the *Pope* giving permission for a particular *Canon* Law to be suspended in particular circumstances.

Infulae (Latin "headband"), the streamers hanging from a *mitre*.

Inquisition (Latin *INQUISITIO* "enquiry"), the *office* charged with inquiring into peoples' complaints against teachers or writers who distort the faith. The Roman Inquisition was later called the *Holy Office*, or the *Congregation* of the Doctrine of the Faith.

Introit (Latin *INTROITUS*, "entry"), the first proper text of the *Mass*; a verse of Scripture to set the theme. The first word of the *Introit* is often used to designate the whole *Mass*, e.g. *Requiem*.

J

Jesuits, An order of *priests* founded by St Ignatius of Loyola in the sixteenth century. They took a special vow, in addition to the usual ones of poverty, chastity and obedience, to put themselves absolutely at the disposal of the *Pope* for the purposes of *mission*. Historically very active in education at all levels; more recently often associated with practical, and sometimes controversial, implementation of the Church's "option for the poor".

K

Knights of St Columba, an association of men devoted to *evangelization* and practical works of charity.

Kyrie (Greek, "O Lord"), a repetitive chant asking for mercy, near the beginning of *Mass*, and often set to music.

L

Lady Day, English traditional name for the *Annunciation*.

Laetare Sunday, the fourth Sunday of *Lent*, when the *Introit* begins Laetare, "rejoice", and the sombre colour of the *vestments* is lightened to a delicate rose.

Laity (Greek *LAOS*, "people"), or *Lay people*, the majority of members of the *Church* who are not set aside as *clergy*.

Last Blessing, traditional term for the blessing given by the *priest* near the end of *Mass*.

Last Gospel, the first verses of St John's *Gospel*, read at the end of the traditional Old Rite Tridentine *Mass*.

Last Rites, Historical term used for *Anointing* given to those near death. No longer an accurate description for the *Anointing of the Sick*, or the *Last Sacraments*.

Last Sacraments, for those about to die, if possible the *priest* gives the *Sacrament* of *Penance*, with *Absolution* and a Plenary *Indulgence*, and *Holy Communion* in the form of *Viaticum*. If the sick person has not yet been Anointed, that may be done too.

Lauds (Latin *LAUDES*, "praises"), the second hour of the *Divine Office*, also known as Morning *Prayer*; psalms including those of praise, and the *Benedictus* or Canticle of Zechariah.

Lavabo (Latin *LAVABO*, "I will wash"), the stage at *Mass* when the *priest* washes his hands, hence the lavabo-basin and the lavabo-towel for his use.

Lay Apostolate, the role of the *laity* in spreading the Faith, consisting in *evangelization* and almsgiving, nourished by *prayer* and study.

Lay people, the *Laity*.

Lectern, a stand to hold the book from which Scripture is read at *Mass*, or the works of the Fathers at *Matins*. May be decorated with a fabric lectern-fall to match the *vestments*. See *Ambo*.

Lectionary (Latin *LECTIO*, "reading"), the book containing the readings from the Bible used at *Mass*.

Lector (Latin, "reader"), originally the second grade of *Holy Orders*, now suspended in the Latin Church. Now used for a lay ministry, assistant to the *priest*, hardly ever conferred except for those on the way to *ordination* as *Deacon* or *Priest*. Also used for those who proclaim the Word of God (reading) in the *Liturgy*, usually at *Mass*.

Legilium, a folding portable *Lectern*.

Legion of Christ, an *order* of *clergy* devoted to *evangelization*.

Legion of Mary, an association of *Lay people* devoted to *evangelization*.

Lent (Middle English LENTEN, "spring"), the *season* of *penance* from Ash Wednesday to *Easter* Sunday, consisting of 40 days.

Litany (Greek LITANEIA "prayer"), a *prayer* consisting of many short invocations with a common response, often used at *Benediction* or during *Exposition*. The most popular is the *Litany* of Loreto, a *litany* invoking the prayers of the Virgin Mary. The *Litany* of the Saints is used at Ordinations.

Little Hours, the four hours of the *Divine Office* in the daytime, *Prime*, *Terce*, *Sext* and *None*, and now, after the liturgical reforms of *Vatican* Council II, subsumed into Prayer during the Day. See *Divine Office*.

Liturgy (Greek *LEITOURGIA*, "public service"), the public worship of the *Church*, in particular the *Mass*, and the way it is conducted. Hence the *Liturgy* of the Word, the first half of the *Mass* featuring the Scripture readings; and *Liturgy* of the *Eucharist*, the second half, with the *Eucharistic Prayer* and *Communion*.

Lourdes, village, now a major Marian shrine, in France associated the with apparition of the Virgin Mary to Bernadette Soubirous in 1858. Commemorated on 11th February.

Low Sunday, traditional English name for the Sunday after *Easter*, sometimes called *Quasimodo Sunday* (after the first word of the Latin *introit* for the *Mass* of the day). The exact origin of the term "Low Sunday" is obscure; as it is the *Octave* day of *Easter*, it may originally have been an analogy from the eight note musical scale (where *Easter* Sunday is the first note). Now also known as *Divine Mercy* Sunday.

M

Madonna (Italian, "my Lady"), term of endearment for the Virgin Mary.

Magisterium (Latin *MAGISTER*, "master" "teacher"), the teaching authority of the *Church*, specifically the *Pope* with his assistants, and General Councils.

Magnificat (Latin, "magnifies"), the canticle of Mary (Lk 1:46-55), used at *Vespers*.

Maniple, the fourth of the *Vestments* for *Mass*, a band of fabric matching the *stole*, worn over the left arm, but now usually omitted.

Martyr (Greek *MARTYS*, "witness"), one who gives witness to the faith by accepting death. To be a *martyr* the person must be confronted with a real choice over whether to abandon the faith or remain loyal.

Mass (Latin *MISSA*, "sending"), the central act of Christian worship, in which, after the reading of Scripture and prayers, the *priest* consecrates the bread and wine to become the *Eucharist*.

Matins (Latin *MATUTINA*, "morning"), sometimes known as *Vigils* or the *Office* of Readings, the first and longest hour of the *Divine Office*, containing psalms and long readings from Scripture or the *Fathers of the Church*. Traditionally celebrated in the night.

Matrimony, the holy *sacrament* by which one man and one woman are joined in lifelong faithfulness, a living parable of the union between Christ and His *Church*.

Maundy Thursday (Latin *MANDATUM*, "commandment'), the Thursday of *Holy Week*, which commemorates the Last Supper, Jesus washing the feet of the Apostles and the New Commandment to love one another (Jn 13-17).

Meditation, mental *prayer* that uses the intellect and reason, pondering on some text of Scripture or point of doctrine, and drawing conclusions.

Memorial, the lowest rank of special days, for minor saints and those of local interest only; some Memorials are Optional, others compulsory.

Metropolitan (Greek *MÉTÉR*, "mother" and *POLIS*, "city"), alternative name for an *Archbishop*, whose seat may be called a *Metropolitan Cathedral*.

Midday prayer, also called Prayer during the Day. Short "hour" of the *Divine Office* celebrated during the day; in the reformed *Breviary*, this single liturgy replaces the old canonical hours of *Terce*, *Sext* and *None*.

Missal, a book containing all the texts of the *Mass*. These include the Ordinary of the *Mass* (also called the Order of Mass) which consists of the unchanging parts (including the *Eucharistic Prayers*); the prayers (*introits*, *collects*, *offertory prayers*, *prefaces*, *post-communion prayers*) for different Sundays and feastdays (these are sometimes called "Propers"); and the Bible readings for Sundays and feastdays taken from the *Lectionary*. Many Catholics will own a small *Missal* for use at Mass. *Priests* saying Mass will often use a *Missal* without the *Lectionary* readings; this is known as an *Altar Missal* or *Sacramentary*.

Mission (Latin *MISSIO*, "sending"), the responsibility of every Christian to bring the Word of God into the world.

Mission (ii), a location from which missionaries (*clergy*, *religious* and *laity*) can begin the work of spreading the Word of God. Once well-established, a *Mission* will become a *Parish*.

Mitre (Persian *MITRA*, "hat"), the distinctive headdress of a *bishop*, rising to a peak in front and behind, and with two streamers or *infulae* hanging down behind.

Monastery (Greek *MONASTÉRION* from *MONOS*, "solitary"), the home of a community of vowed *monks* or *nuns*.

Monk (Greek *MONACHOS* from *MONOS*, "solitary"), a man who dedicates his life to *prayer*, taking *vows* to remain in the same place for life, under *obedience*, and living as befits a *monk*, that is without owning anything as an individual (*poverty*) and in *continence* (*chastity*).

Monsignor (French *MON SEIGNEUR*, "my superior"), courtesy title for various grades of *prelate*, in England used only for those below the rank of *Bishop*.

Monstrance (Latin *MONSTRANTIA* "a showing"), a stand, usually shaped like a rayed sun, to contain and display the *Blessed Sacrament* during *Benediction* and *Exposition*.

Morning Prayer, alternative name for *Lauds*.

Mother of God, a *Solemnity* replacing the *Circumcision* on the 1st of January. Reference to Mary, mother of Jesus.

Motu Proprio (Latin "on his own initiative"), a letter from the *Pope* making a decision on some minor matter.

Mozetta, a fur-lined shoulder cape worn by *canons*.

Mystery (Greek *MYSTERION*, "secret"), something unknown to the Old Testament and to the pagans but now revealed in the *Church*. Often used to mean something beyond the power of mere human reason to work out, hence needing to be taught by God.

Mystery (ii), an aspect of the life of Christ chosen as a subject for *meditation*, especially in the *Rosary*.

Mystical Body of Christ, the *Church* considered as being formed by the *Eucharist*, and forming the *Eucharist*.

N

None (Latin *NONUS*, "ninth"), the sixth hour of the older *Divine Office*, for the ninth hour after daybreak. See *Midday prayer*.

Nôtre Dame, French for *Our Lady*, being a reference to Mary, mother of Jesus.

Novena (Latin *NOVEM*, "nine") a *prayer* or devotion carried on for nine successive days, or weeks, or months. Prototype is the nine days between *Ascension* Thursday and *Pentecost* Sunday.

Nun (Latin *NONNA*, "granny"), a woman who lives a life of *prayer*, equivalent to a *monk*.

Nunc Dimittis (Latin, "now thou dost dismiss"), the canticle of Simeon (Lk 2:29-35), used at *Compline*.

O

Obedience, as a religious virtue or vow, the commitment to follow the instructions of the superior of a *monastery* or other *religious* institution.

Octave (Latin *OCTAVUS*, "eighth"), the custom of extending a major occasion throughout the succeeding eight days, formerly kept for all Solemnities, at present only *Christmas* and *Easter*.

Offertory, the action of presenting bread and wine at *Mass*, hence the *Offertory* Prayers that go with this, and the *Offertory* verse, sung to accompany it.

Offertory (ii), the collection of money usually taken during the *Offertory* at *Mass*.

Office, familiar term for the *Divine Office*.

Office of Readings, alternative name for *Matins*.

Ombrellino (Italian, "umbrella'), a fabric umbrella carried over the *Blessed Sacrament* during indoor *processions*, e.g. on *Corpus Christi*.

Opening Prayer, term for *Collect*.

Opus Dei (Latin "work of God"), traditional term for the *Divine Office*, especially as sung in Benedictine monasteries.

Opus Dei (ii), an organization of *Lay people* dedicated to growth in holiness, served by *priests* of the Society of the Holy Cross, and founded by St Josemaria Escriva.

Oratory, a place of *prayer* which does not contain an altar; sometimes used for any *chapel*.

Oratory (ii), a spiritual exercise of prayers, readings, preaching and music founded by St Philip Neri to help the *laity* to pray. The *Congregation* of the *Oratory* was instituted to conduct these exercises.

Order, Holy, the various grades of service to God and the *Church*, originally consisting of seven orders, now generally confined to three, *Deacon*, *Priest* and *Bishop*.

Order, Religious, a national or international organization of *monks*, *nuns*, *clerks* etc dedicated to *prayer* or *mission*. Every *Order* has its own distinctive *charism*, purpose, or service.

Ordinary Time, "Ordinary" here means "numbered, ordered", from the Latin *ORDINARIUS*. It refers to those weeks of the liturgical year which do not fall within the *seasons* of *Advent*, *Christmas*, *Lent*, or *Easter*, and include a period of around 34 numbered weeks. Sometimes known as "Time through the Year".

Ordination, the conferring of the status of *Deacon*, *Priest* or *Bishop* by *prayer* and the laying on of hands, to *consecrate* them for sacred duties; performed only by a *bishop*.

Orphrey (French *ORFÈVRERIE*, "goldsmith's work"), a strip of decorated fabric, used to adorn *vestments*, such as the *chasuble* and *dalmatic*, and the altar-frontal.

Our Lady, common Catholic way of referring to Mary, the mother of Jesus; also Blessed Virgin Mary.

Our Lord, usual Catholic way of referring to Jesus Christ.

P

Pall, a small square of stiffened fabric, used to cover the *chalice* to keep dust and flies out of it.

Pall (ii), a large fabric cover to drape over a coffin, traditionally black. Hence pall-bearers who walk beside the coffin.

Palm, a branch of palm or other greenery (traditionally the pussy-willow, but now usually a real *palm* frond). Palms, as an evergreen, are an ancient Christian symbol of the resurrection to eternal life.

Palm Sunday, the Sunday beginning Holy Week, also known as *Passion Sunday*. So called because traditionally on that day *palm* fronds are carried in procession to commemorate Jesus's triumphal entry into Jerusalem (Mk 11:1-10).

Parish (Greek PAR' OIKIA, "around the house"), the smallest unit of territory in the *Church*, centered on a single *church* and served by a *priest* as **Parish Priest** (in America, Pastor), with one or more assistants or curates, living in a *presbytery*.

Pasch (Hebrew PESACH, "passover'), *Easter*, hence Paschaltide, the *Easter Season*, and Paschal Candle, a great candle blessed at the *Easter Vigil* and kept on the *Sanctuary*, traditionally until the *Ascension*, now at least until *Pentecost* if not all year round.

Passion, the narrative of the suffering and death of Jesus, read solemnly on *Palm Sunday* and *Good Friday*.

Passion Sunday, traditionally two weeks before *Easter*, when the mood of *Lent* changes from one of *penance* to a time to meditate on the *passion* of Christ in Passiontide; now used as a synonym for *Palm Sunday*.

Pastoral staff, or *crosier*, a long staff or metal or wood, topped with a curled head like a shepherd's crook, carried by *bishops* and *abbots* as a symbol of their pastoral care.

Paten, a plate of gold or gilt silver, used for the bread which is to be consecrated at *Mass*.

Pater noster (Latin "Our Father"), Latin form of the Lord's Prayer (Mt 6:9-13), which Jesus taught to his disciples.

Patron Saint, the saint who is particularly honoured in a specific nation, city or *parish*, or for a particular group of people; e.g. Ss Cosmas and Damian for doctors, St Patrick for Ireland.

Penance (Latin *PAENITENTIA*, "turning back"), the acceptance that we have failed in sin, and the firm resolve to make a fresh start, best expressed in the *Sacrament* of *Penance*, or *Reconciliation*, *Confession*.

Penance (ii), a *prayer* recited, an action undertaken, or a suffering willingly accepted, to demonstrate the sincerity of sorrow for sin, and a wish to share in the saving work of Christ. Traditionally *Penance* consists of *Prayer*, *Fasting* and *Almsgiving*.

Penitential Rite, a preliminary part of the *Mass* including the admission of guilt and confident *prayer* for forgiveness.

Pentecost, (Greek *PENTEKOSTÉ*, "fiftieth"), Sunday fifty days after *Easter* Sunday concluding the season of Easter. It commemorates the descent of the Holy Spirit on the Apostles & the Virgin Mary (Ac 2:1-13), which took place on the Jewish feast of *Pentecost*. This feast, fifty days after the first day of Passover, is also called the Feast of Weeks; as well as being a harvest festival, in Jewish tradition it also commemorates the revelation of the Torah to Moses on Mount Sinai. The Holy Spirit's descent in the form of tongues of fire reminds us of God's descent in fire and smoke on Sinai (Ex 19:18).

Pontiff (Latin *PONTIFEX*, "bridge-builder"), a title of the *Pope* (the Supreme Pontiff), but also extended as an adjective, *pontifical*, to all *bishops*.

Pontifical, the book containing the special ceremonies for which a *Bishop* is responsible.

Poor Clares, an *Order* of *Nuns* living in *poverty*, inspired by St Clare, the friend of St Francis.

Pope (Latin *PAPA*, "daddy"), the *Bishop* of Rome, chosen by the *Cardinals* to act as focus of unity and guarantee of truth for the entire *Church*.

Porter (Latin *PORTA*, "door"), originally the fourth grade of *Holy Orders*, now suspended in the Latin Church. The responsibility was to guard the *church* door.

Post-Communion, traditional term for the *Prayer after Communion* at *Mass*.

Poverty, as a religious virtue or vow, among *monks* the commitment not to claim ownership of anything personally.

Prayer, the "lifting up of heart and soul to God", which must be both public, in the *Mass* and other ceremonies, and private, in the privacy of the home. Private *prayer* may be vocal (using words) or mental; the latter either meditative or contemplative.

Prayer after Communion, the *prayer* recited by the *priest* after *Communion* at *Mass*, formerly called the *Post-communion*.

Prayer of the Faithful, the intercessions made at *Mass* after the *sermon*, otherwise *Bidding Prayers*.

Prayer over the Gifts, the *prayer* recited by the *priest* after the *Offertory* at *Mass*, formerly called the *Secret*.

Preach (Latin *PRAE DICERE*, "speak out"), to deliver an authoritative address instructing the faithful, usually at *Mass*. The preserve of *priests* and *deacons*, most of whose long training is preparation for preaching.

Preface, a thanksgiving *prayer* immediately preceding the *Eucharistic Prayer* at *Mass*.

Prelate (Latin *PRAE LATUS*, "put forward"), a senior member of the *clergy*; some are nominally members of the Papal household (Prelates of Honour, Domestic Prelates, or Protonotaries Apostolic), usually known as *Monsignori* in England; *Bishops* and Abbots are also *prelates*.

Premonstratentians (French place name, *PRÉMONTRÉ*), an *order* of Canons Regular founded by St Norbert, who wear white *habits*.

Presbytery (Greek *PRESBYTEROS*, "elder"), the house where the *parish priest* and curates live, adjacent to the *parish Church*. In America known as a rectory.

Presentation of the Lord, the feast on 2nd February (formerly called the *Purification*, or *Candlemas*), commemorating the Presentation of the infant Jesus by his parents in the Temple (Lk 2:22-38).

Priest (Greek *PRESBYTEROS*, "elder"), a man set aside to serve God and the *Church* through *ordination*, with the particular power to hear *confessions*, anoint the sick, and to celebrate *Mass*. In the Western Church expected to be unmarried and live in *continence* or *celibacy*.

Prime (Latin *PRIMA HORA*, "first hour"), the third hour of the *Divine Office*, at the first hour of daylight, now generally omitted. See *Divine Office*; *Midday Prayer*.

Prior, and **Prioress**, the second-in-command of a large *monastery* or abbey; also the one in charge of a small *monastery* or Priory.

Procession, a devotional exercise consisting in people walking (processing) solemnly in line, either around a *church* or from one *church* to another, sometimes carrying the *Blessed Sacrament*, or a statue or banners. Often a feature of the *solemnity* of *Corpus Christi*, and certain Marian devotions, and *Good Friday*.

Protonotary Apostolic (Greek *PROTOS* "first" and Latin *NOTARIUS* "secretary"), originally a senior secretary to the *Pope*, now the highest grade of honorary *prelate* or *monsignor* below a *bishop*.

Province, an area of territory consisting of several *dioceses*, headed by an *Archbishop*.

Provost (Latin *PRAEPOSITUS*, "set in charge"), the superior of a community of *canons*, or a *Congregation* of the *Oratory*.

Pulpit (Latin *PULPITUM* "platform"), a high raised platform, with enclosing rail, for preaching situated so that the preacher is easily visible from all parts of the *church*.

Purification, the process of cleaning the *Paten* and *Chalice* after *Mass*, to ensure that no crumbs or drops of the *Eucharist* remain. The *Chalice* is wiped and dried with a Purificator, a white folded rectangle of linen.

Purification (ii), traditional name for the feast on 2nd February, commemorating the ceremony when Mary came to give thanks for her Childbirth, and the infant Jesus was presented in the Temple, otherwise called *Candlemas*.

Pyx (Greek *PYXIS* "box"), a small round airtight container for carrying a consecrated *host* to give *Communion* to the sick.

Q

Quadragesima (Latin "40th"), the *season* of *Lent*, comprising 40 days until *Easter*.

Quarant'ore, Italian for *Forty Hours* devotion.

Quasimodo (Sunday) (Latin, "in the manner of"), the Sunday after *Easter* Sunday when the *Introit* begins "in the manner of new born infants" and so named. In England called *Low Sunday*.

Quinquagesima (Latin "50th"), in the traditional calendar the Sunday before *Lent*, (50 days before *Holy Saturday*).

R

RCIA, Acronym for Rite of Christian Initiation of Adults, properly the title of a book of ceremonies for receiving adult converts, commonly used to mean the *Catechumenate*.

Reconciliation, process of making up differences, forgiving and being forgiven. Refers also to the *Sacrament* of *Reconciliation*, or of *Penance*, also known as *Confession*.

Reliquary, a container used to house and display a relic of a saint.

Rector (Latin "ruler"), little-used word for a *priest* with responsibility for a *church*, but in America Rectory is commonly used for a *Presbytery*.

Religious (Latin *RELIGIO*, "binding together"), members of an *Order* of *monks*, *nuns*, *clerks* etc, as distinguished from secular *clergy*.

Requiem (Latin, "rest"), a *Mass* for the Dead, named after the first word in the *Introit*.

Reservation of the Blessed Sacrament, keeping some of the consecrated *Eucharist* in the form of bread in a *Tabernacle*, so that it is available for *Communion* of the sick, and for adoration.

Rochet, similar to the *surplice* but with narrow sleeves worn by *canons* and *prelates*.

Rosary, (Latin *ROSARIUM* "rose garden"), a traditional form of prayer to the Virgin Mary. It is usually recited on a *chaplet* of beads (called rosary beads, or often just a rosary). Its basic pattern is called a decade (each one Our Father, ten Hail Marys, and one Glory Be). Each decade is assigned to a particular episode (called a mystery) from the New Testament, dealing with the life of Christ and the Virgin Mary, which is meditated on whilst the prayers are said. There are twenty mysteries in all, arranged in four groups of five (Joyful, Luminous, Sorrowful, and Glorious).

S

Sacrament (Latin SACRAMENTUM from SACRARE, "consecrate"), one of seven ceremonies instituted by Christ and used in the *Church* to bring people into contact with God in different ways: *Baptism* and *Confirmation* as initiation, *Eucharist* for incorporation into the Body of Christ, and for regular nourishment; *Ordination* or *Matrimony* for Christian *mission*, *Penance* and *Anointing of the Sick* for when things go wrong.

Sacramentary, a book containing the various prayers for *Mass* without the Bible readings; also called an *Altar Missal*. See also *Missal*.

Sacred Heart, the Friday after the second Sunday after *Pentecost*, a *Solemnity* to celebrate the human love of God for us, expressed in the heart of Jesus.

Saints' days, days commemorating particular saints, usually the anniversary of the day they died; major ones are commemorated world-wide, as *Solemnities*, *Feasts* or *Memorials*; others have only local commemorations. On every day of the year there are many saints to commemorate, so not all can be kept anywhere.

Saint Joseph, spouse of Mary the mother of Jesus; *Solemnity* on 19th March.

Saint Peter and Saint Paul, a *Solemnity* on 29th June. Peter, apostle and first Pope; Paul great evangelizer and author of many of the New Testament Letters.

Sanctuary, the area of the *church* around the altar, set aside for ceremonial worship; containing the altar and traditionally demarcated by steps and altar-rails.

Sanctuary lamp, a white or red lamp kept burning near the *Tabernacle* to indicate that the *Blessed Sacrament* is reserved there.

Sanctus (Latin "holy"), the text between the *Preface* and the *Eucharistic Prayer* at *Mass*, often set to music.

Scrutiny, the ceremonial examination of *Catechumens* before *Baptism*, sometimes conducted publicly on Sundays in *Lent*.

Seasons, liturgical, the divisions of the year into periods when Christians particularly meditate on certain aspects of salvation: these are now *Advent*, *Christmas Season*, *Lent*, and Eastertide.

Secret, old name for the *Prayer over the Gifts*, always said silently.

Seculars (Latin *SAECULUM*, "world"), those in the world, in particular *priests* who have a *mission* to the world.

See (Latin *SEDES*, "seat"), the seat of a *bishop*, hence his *Diocese*. The *Holy See* is the *Diocese* of Rome.

Seminary (Latin *SEMINARE*, "sow seed"), a training college for *priests*, ideally situated adjacent to the *Cathedral* and the *bishop*'s residence. A Junior *Seminary* (in America, Minor *Seminary*) is for boys who would otherwise be unable to receive adequate education in adolescence; a Major *Seminary* for those over 18.

Septuagesima (Latin "70th"), in the traditional calendar the Sunday three weeks before *Lent*, (70 days before *Low Sunday*).

Sequence, a long verse hymn sung before the *Gospel* at *Mass* on certain special days.

Sermon (Latin *SERMO*, "speech"), a discourse in which the *priest* explains the readings at *Mass*.

Sexagesima (Latin "60th"), in the traditional calendar the Sunday two weeks before *Lent*, (60 days before *Easter* Wednesday).

Sext (Latin SEXTUS, "sixth"), the fifth hour of the older *Divine Office*, for the sixth hour after daybreak, or midday. See *Midday prayer*.

Shrove Tuesday (Middle English, SCHRIVE, "give Absolution"), the day before *Ash Wednesday*, when all should receive the *Sacrament* of *Penance* as a preparation for *Lent*. Traditionally marked by using up the meat and dairy products from which people fasted, and therefore called "fat Tuesday" (MARDI GRAS) etc.), or "goodbye meat", CARNE VALE, (carnival).

Society of St Vincent de Paul, an association of *Lay people* devoted to practical works of charity.

Solemnity, the highest rank of special days, for really important saints (including the local patron), and events in the life of Jesus.

Stations of the Cross (Latin STATIO, "stopping place"), a devotion following in imagination the walk of Jesus from the court of Pontius Pilate to the hill of Calvary, with fourteen "stations" based on sites in Jerusalem where certain events are believed to have occurred. Representations or symbols of the Stations are usually arranged around the walls of churches.

Stole (Greek *STOLÉ*, "garment"), the fifth of the *Vestments* for *Mass*, a band of fabric, usually fringed, and of a colour and design to match the *Chasuble* (and *Maniple*, if used), worn round the neck and hanging down in front. Traditionally it was crossed on the breast, except by *bishops*. It is worn over the left shoulder by *deacons*. Also used over a *Surplice* when administering the *sacraments* of *Baptism*, *Penance* and *Anointing*. A miniature *stole* is used for administering *Communion* and *Anointing* in homes or hospitals. Its origins are unclear but probably lie in the scarf of office worn by Roman Imperial officials.

Subdeacon, a grade of *Holy Order* below *deacon*, at present suspended in the Western Rite.

Surplice, a light garment of white fabric with wide sleeves, closed at the front, worn over the *cassock*.

SVP, the *Society of St Vincent de Paul*.

Synod (Greek *SYNODOS*, "council"), a meeting of *bishops*, usually for one nation or region (local *Synod*). The *Synod* of *Bishops* meets regularly in Rome as an advisory body to the *Pope*.

T

Tabernacle (Latin *TABERNACULUM*, "tent"), a secure strong fixed container for reserving the *Blessed Sacrament*, in a church or chapel, indicated by a *Sanctuary lamp* and covered with a *tabernacle* veil of the colour of the *season*.

Tenebrae (Latin, "darkness"), old name for *Matins* and *Lauds* of *Maundy Thursday*, *Good Friday* and *Holy Saturday*, formerly sung in darkness with dramatic effect.

Terce (Latin *TERTIUS*, "third"), the fourth hour of the older *Divine Office*, for the third hour after daybreak. See *Midday prayer*.

Thurible (Latin *THUS*, from Greek *THYOS* "incense"), or *censer*, a metal container suspended from chains, used for burning *incense*.

Tonsure (Latin *TONSURA*, "shaving"), shaving the crown of the head, originally the distinguishing mark of all *clergy*, now used only among certain orders of *monks* and *friars*.

Tract, a chant traditionally used just before the *Gospel* at *Mass* during *Lent*, when the Alleluia chant is omitted.

Tradition (Latin *TRADERE*, "pass on"), the duty of faithfully passing on to the next generation what we have received from the past (Tt 1:9), hence the ever-developing body of Catholic teaching, or *Deposit of Faith*.

Transfiguration, feast kept on 6th August to celebrate the Transfiguration of Jesus (Mk 9:2-8).

Triduum (Latin "three days"), three days at the end of *Holy Week* during which the entire *Easter* mystery is celebrated in its fullness in an extended series of liturgies from *Maundy Thursday* to *Good Friday*, *Holy Saturday* and the *Easter Vigil*. The greatest feast in the Christian calendar.

Trinity Sunday, the first Sunday after *Pentecost*, a *solemnity* to meditate on the nature of God, Three in One.

Tunicle (Latin *TUNICULA*, "little tunic"), a garment almost identical to the *Dalmatic*, worn by the *Subdeacon* at *Mass*.

V

Vatican, a hill near Rome, the usual residence of the Pope. Although wholly surrounded by the city of Rome proper, it is in fact a separate sovereign state, formally the Vatican City State, with its own laws, police force, armed forces, post office &c. Also used as shorthand or casually to refer to the *Papacy* or *Holy See*.

Vespers (Latin *VESPERAE*, "evening"), the seventh hour of the *Divine Office*, also known as Evening *Prayer*; psalms including those of praise, and the *Magnificat* or Canticle of Mary.

Vestments, the garments worn by *clergy* and assistants for *Mass* and other ceremonies. (A full set of *Vestments* comprises the *chasuble*, *stole*, *maniple*, *burse*, chalice veil, tabernacle veil, lectern fall and altar-frontal, supplemented with *dalmatic*, *tunicle* and *Humeral veil* to make a traditional "High Mass set".)

Viaticum (Latin, "food for the journey"), the *sacrament* of *Holy Communion* given to those about to die.

Vicar (Latin *VICARIUS*, "deputy"), an official with delegated authority, thus a Vicar Apostolic is delegated by the *Pope* to serve an area which has not yet been structured as a *diocese*; a Vicar General is the *bishop's* deputy for all matters, a Vicar Judicial his deputy for legal matters, a Vicar Episcopal may look after an area within a *diocese*.

Vigil, Vigils (Latin *VIGILIAE*, "keeping watch"), generally, a vigil is praying during the night. *Vigils* is a name for the hour of *Matins* (the *Office of Readings* from the *Divine Office*) used by some monastic orders (such as the *Carthusians*) who celebrate it during the night. The *Easter*

Vigil is the culmination of the *Triduum*, opening the season of *Easter*. In the early Church, it was celebrated during the night, ending with the *Eucharist* at dawn. After the liturgical renewal following the Second Vatican Council, the Church has encouraged the recovery of this way of celebrating the *Easter Vigil*. See also *Vigil Mass*.

Vigil Mass, *mass* for a Sunday or feast day celebrated on the evening beforehand; this expresses the Church's understanding of time, drawn from the Jewish tradition, whereby a day runs from sunset to sunset (thus, Sunday begins liturgically on Saturday evening).

Visitation, feast kept on 31st May to commemorate the visit of Mary mother of Jesus to Elizabeth her cousin (Lk 1:39-56).

Vow, a solemn promise made to God before witnesses.

W

Whitefriars, traditional English name for *Carmelites*.

Z

Zucchetto, a round skull cap, black for *priests*, purple for *prelates*, red for *cardinals* and white for the *Pope*.

Informative Catholic Reading

We hope that you have enjoyed reading this booklet.

If you would like to find out more about CTS booklets - we'll send you our free information pack and catalogue.

Please send us your details:

Name ....

Address ....

....

....

Postcode ....

Telephone ....

Email ....

Send to: CTS, 40-46 Harleyford Road,
Vauxhall, London
SE11 5AY

Tel: 020 7640 0042
Fax: 020 7640 0046
Email: info@cts-online.org.uk

CTS